The Qi of G

Poetic pieces on life, love & other cosmic curiosities.

Garth Sam © 2019

This book is dedicated to two people.

First, to my mother Catherine whose steadfast love, strength, faith & support have empowered me to not only live an exceptional life, but also to help others do likewise.

Second, to my brother-in-law Derek Taylor who died unexpectedly & far too soon on Mar, 12, 2019. I know Derek would have been honestly happy to see my words published.

Acknowledgements

Over the years more than a handful of people have encouraged me to share my writing, so this book at last -pays humble homage to the synergy of those kind voices. More specifically however, I am eager to make sure that the following small-circle of people know how much I appreciate their sincere support for my writing, as well as their positive presence in my life overall.

Thank you Vishnu Ramdeen for being such a steadfast & stalwart best friend who has always supported my unconventional m.o....even if it didn't seem to make much sense or many dollars. Your success in business speaks volumes as a testimony to your mantra "success by determination", but over the years I've been most proud to watch you grow into the dedicated dad that you have become to your 3 children. Bravo brother.

Thank you Wendy St. Cyr for 30 plus years of happily enjoying & encouraging my eclectic lifedance in faith that your favorite Peter Pan was simply destined to romp down roads less travelled. Who would have thunk it all those years ago that I might prove to be not quite so "brainless but cute"? Lol: you I guess.

Thank you Dana Reiter for being a truly refreshing bright light to me as a fellow global adventurer, intrepid outlier & one of the most unpretentiously wonder-full people I know. Moreover, I love *your* writing & can't wait until you give more people a chance to enjoy the magical gifts that flow from *your* pen.

Next, a very BIG & special THANK YOU to my sister Dr. Lanalee Araba Sam for not only sharing a lifetime of memories & moments with me, but also for really leaning-in to make this book a reality. I am forever grateful for your generosity, dedicated efforts as my editor plus on this project & loving reminders that "done is better than perfect". From womb to tomb with this paper product in hand dear wondertwin, merci beaucoup!

Last but definitely not least, muchas gracias to my beloved yinmate T'ameaux who has been a powerfully patient, uniquely intuitive & dynamically delicious tour de force beside me for over a decade now, as I have sauntered slooooowly towards publishing this first book. Thank you mi amor for everything you have done & continue to do, to support my best be-ing as an evolutionary Man & your life partner. May we continue to thrive happily together as complementary life artistes!

Contents

Foreword

My passion for more than 60 years has been to explore the world both the physical world with its diverse communities, and the world of ideas which I have found to be equally diverse.

Shortly after my 80th birthday I was introduced to Garth Sam with whom I felt an immediate kinship. Although separated in age by 30 years, we shared many remarkable similarities in terms of the way we were enjoying our uncommonly dynamic journeys.

We both approached life with the perspective of open-minded Explorers, we held very similar values and priorities, and we also discovered that we had many common friends not only in North America but also in Africa.

Like myself I also found that Garth was enthusiastic about personal expeditions in search of best practices to develop effective leadership, nurture cross-cultural harmony and drive high performance. This aligned further with our mutual interest in building inspired collaborative networks to facilitate sustainable prosperity in local communities and around the world.

Garth subsequently invited me to serve as an elder in his growing fraternal organization, The Universal Brotherhood (aka TUB) which I was happy to do given its auspicious nutshell mission of "building bonds & better Men". I was especially intrigued by the succinct but powerful platform he was developing for Men based on the 5 key TUB

Foundations of Strength, Wisdom, Integrity, Prosperity & Compassion.

Through my involvement with the TUB Network both in Canada and the USA I came to respect the depth of Garth's personal philosophy, as well as his impressive ability to articulate his thoughts with both style and substance. Moreover, I learned that he often used creative writing as a medium for expression, and was honored when he presented me with a framed, "DNA-certified" copy of the poem "Weighs & Means" which is included in this collection.

Then on the evening of November 23rd, as I was preparing to fly to Nairobi, Garth sent me a digital version of this publication along with the surprise request to write an introduction for it. Being a man who would rather show first than tell, Garth had only revealed that he was working on this book 24 hours earlier, but I was unaware of its contents.

I immediately reviewed the book on the overnight flight to Kenya and my first reaction was one of big surprise. Initially I felt like I was being overwhelmed by an avalanche of Garth's creative energy and I was astounded by the number, the range of themes, and the insightful power of the poems Garth was preparing to share. Clearly, I was being introduced to yet another intriguing aspect of my wonderful multi-faceted friend.

As I carried on with my Kenyan trip, I continued to review Garth's pieces and to absorb the inspiring impact of his first published collection. Garth is undeniably a talented writer whose work is personal, provocative, profound and often gracefully sublime. Suffice it to say that I have been moved emotionally and intellectually by this literary experience which has opened up a whole new range of tantalizing topics for Garth and I to discuss in the months ahead.

I invite you to join me in exploring the powerful thoughts of this calm, strong, thoughtful and compassionate modern-day renaissance leader.

Let The Journey Continue!

Don Simpson, PhD.
Chief Explorer
The Renaissance Expedition
Nairobi, Dec. 10th, 2019

Preface

Thank you for reading these words and any others that attract your eyes in this book. Truth be told, I've been slow to share my writing, but in the wake of much well-meant prodding by various people who have enjoyed nibbles of my scribbles, you now have a sneak peek into the eclectic musings of yours truly. Within these pages is a mixed bag of bits that were written at different places & chapters in my adult life. Each piece tells its own tale, inspired by whatever thoughts emotions, or experiences I felt compelled to capture at the time, but I've curated this first collection into five broad thematic sections that I felt were relevant.

Ultimately, you will find that my compositions are a curious reflection of the way my mind wonders and wanders. Moreover, if you are an artist of any kind you will appreciate that sometimes you feel like you are the contemplative master creator, but many times things simply come to you & through you. As far as a process is concerned then, much of my writing here feels very "top-down" to me too & I am often left wondering where the words "came from".

That said, I like the humbling idea of being more-than-less a convenient conduit for images from the ether, rather than just a self-reliant wordsmith. The piece "Destiny Divined" combines these two aspects of uncertain origination perfectly for me with the following favorite line, "Is there truly a beginning or do I just offer back, the brittle verses of another who the hands and means do lack?". Whatever the case and for what its worth, at the end of the day the words you read on these pages all flowed from my hands which means I get to call myself their author. Now it remains to be seen if anything I've written resonates with you as interesting, odd or inspiring.

If so, I'll be happy to take credit for those frozen letters & pat myself on the back for putting fingers to keyboard. If not, I say we blame the universe for tricking me into thinking that I had some worthwhile words to share.

Either way, nuff said and life goes on. Please take your time, chew more than once for best digestion, and savor a slice of this man's merry madness.

Garth Sam
Dec. 2019

First Expressions

One mission statement

The goal of the wordsmith:

To extract from ether a collection of courageous impressions

United in authenticity by the yearning of a pregnant moment

Such that every peerless pen-stroke conjures fresh images

That tantalize even as they terrify

Dancing between bliss & brutality

Serenity & lust

Inspiration & despair

Or feelings too subtle for such simple labels

Until the reader surrenders to a dynamic new dreamscape

That comes to life as a perfect tapestry

of shameless provocation.

green

now shaken from slumber

like phoenix reborn

root sightless with hunger

earth blanket is torn

up strong from the darkness

awake through the night

pure instinct productive

genetic the might

As tip cracks the surface

triumphant at last

bold freedom discovered

forsaking the past

anointed by heaven

with new eyes are seen

Sun's beauty eternal:

the promise of green.

Bright Secrets

The sun kissed my cheek this morning
A warm wake-up call to jumpstart the day
As a smile found my promises waiting
I heard a voice deep within my heart say:

Rise inspired and be rightly united
In a marriage of mind, body, and soul
For your destiny is now sweetly calling
There before you the ultimate goal.

An invitation so perfectly tendered
Parting of clouds making blue skies clear
Thus my purpose revealed is remembered
As 8 noble steps bring tranquility near.

So I walk to the beat of my drummer
Feel the rhythm enlightening me
One bright secret speaks louder than thunder
If you listen to Love you will see.

Write or wrong

Some scribble passionately about what they know,
offering naked minds a wardrobe of stylish thoughts to wear.

Others like to tease the mental tines of contemplation,
with ripe dreams & curious mysteries.

The exceptional wordsmith may hammer letters into legends that
survive long after their muses have been forgotten

While avatars & prophets sow virtuous seeds with words of
noble guidance.

I imagine my pen as yet another worthy inksabre,
honed by heart-leanings & ready for battle.

At its best however this is no venal talent for sale
to those who would co-opt an author's gifts.

The world has had enough of malevolent tropes
that divide & conquer,

Whereas I seek to wield language that rends barriers
& builds bonds.

So let me join the a-mused outliers whose potent prose
helps to harmonize humanity.

I know that all great masters of meaning have
the ability to manipulate media

As in turn all true masters of media have the tools
to manipulate meaning.

The world is best when we honor poets whose magical
metaphors inspire & enlighten

And while at times it may be difficult for us to see
when we are wrong

The right words written at the right time
will always have the means
to move the world.

MIRROR IMAGE

we grow by force, if not by choice

encouraged by an inner voice

that prods us on towards the truth

obscured by innocence and youth

though ever-present while we sleep

the treasures of the fertile deep

awaiting ready minds of all

who heed the silent mirror call

to look beyond the bounce of light

reflected first for simple sight

and see the honest face of soul

for this remains the greatest goal.

Dream Life

I dreamed I was a poet
A man with words as pure as silence
And the gift to paint with rainbows
Sights and stories for the soul.

I dreamed I was a poet
A mystic tribesman robed in verses
Songs of sand dunes shifting through me
Rich with wisdom, peace, and hope.

I dreamed I was a poet
On a journey to Atlantis
Chasing mermaids over starfish
Seeking only sacred fruit.

I dreamed I was a poet
Stitching snowflakes into memories
Sculpting moments into magic
Ever-faithful to my art

I dreamed I was a poet
Born to never be restricted
By a world of walls and boxes
Free to savor what I've learned

I dreamed I was a poet
Fertile wordsmith drunk on letters
Spilling ink with sweet abandon
Kissing pages with my angst.

I dreamed I was a poet
Loyal friend to midnight seekers
Lovers, lost, and true believers
Humble signpost of the heart.

I dreamed I was a poet
Hot with lust and thick with passion
All my senses spun together
Claiming ecstasy at night

I dreamed I was a poet
Brave and focused on transition
In the name of evolution
To a wider state of grace.

I dreamed I was a poet
Bound and beaten as a martyr
For the sin of sharing visions
Steeped in universal truth.

I dreamed I was a poet
More than body, sound vibrations
Called to tickle sides of darkness
Humble feather dance of light.

I dreamed I was a poet
Like so many here before me
Finding beauty in allusion
And delight in cosmic mime.

I dreamed I was a poet
And my mind was filled with voices
Everlasting, all forgiving
Singing symphonies of love.

I dreamed I was a poet
Was I dreamt or was I dreaming?
And awoke to find the evening
Turned my in-sight into ink.

True Paradise Lost

Afloat within your gentle yolk, you dream of visions never seen
and nothing that comes after this, shall match the place that you have been.
Perpetual eclipse describes the days that gently blend with night:
uncolored by the world without, the rainbow of your inner sight.
Alone, no other time affords this easy universe of grace
with you the silent tenant of sweet amniotic microspace.
Soul-free & dressed in innocence, unchallenged future-perfect mime:
shame foreign as the concepts both, of avarice & carnal crime.
You celebrate a union which, defines the fluid-perfect fit
no one shall ever claim again, though earnest hearts to each commit.
All edgeless & all intimate, unshifted by Pandora's box
security in naked trust, no worries shake your liquid locks.
Nor seven sins that jaded cast, with tears for every guilty breath
in one-ness with the source of life, so close & yet so far from death.
A fragile bliss in your cocoon, awaiting the impending fall
as nature proves yet once again, that Eden heeds her fertile call.
For it was not the Garden which, the apple's lure all mankind cost
but paradise within the womb, that you & all at birth have lost.

DESTINY DIVINED

This midnight it makes me tired & seems to last so very long.

My thoughts are uninspired, but my words are never wrong.

A victim of the night mood, I feel safe here from my bed.

Vigilante, moonstruck outlaw, living dreams I share instead.

Is there truly a beginning or do I just offer back,

The brittle verses of another who the hands and means do lack?

Grant me total inspiration, visionary to the core,

And I fear my bond to mankind will be lost forever more.

Art, you see, she is my lover, & demand of me she must,

Slavish visions of dark magic, moonlight madness, candid trust.

For the guise that I embrace is neither devilish nor brave,

But instead it is the only fate this troubled heart will crave.

silence

I savor sound but treasure most the silence
it steers me in so many different ways
A thought withheld, a timid breath of violence
the voice unheard yet never disobeyed.

Between the space so many find amusing
there hides a brittle ghost of captive light
and though the echo may be quite confusing
sweet silence is the key to second sight.

Sucker punch

I crawled out of a cold brick box

feeling pale, bleary and crumpled,

a tired fragment of who I once was,

just 8 hours earlier

And then

WHAM!

Ambushed by a golden giant

and slapped silly with a sunbeam.

Sweet solar beatdown:

I never knew *__that__*

could feel *__so__* good!

Process of Illumination

I struggle to embrace visions altogether bizarre

Dream-worthy images clothed in fractured memorabilia

& culled from yesterday's craggy peaks and valleys.

There, in the resting place of all that came before,

The past sows its seeds of inspiration & loss.

From the fertile grave come masterful gleanings

& we are always entertained by

the immortal flavors of timeless angst.

The eyes of the unrequited

Reflect my light clearly that I may be guided
To see of myself who I'm best meant to be;
Infuse me with wisdom & raise me inspired
To honor the grace that resides within me.

Let past marry present & cradle the future
For beauty is born in the bosom of youth
The eyes of a child shine with honor & promise
Like mirrors in sunlight reflecting the truth.

Lit

I am blessed with a unified purpose
Fully bound to the calling of Light
Though I sway I return to the center
Where my fate is to challenge the night.

Equidistant the space all around me
thus I draw in a breath from the whole
As I stretch space to shine in the darkness
time consumes me yet flatters my goal.

Liquid moments that tease me are fragile
complementing the rhymes that I sing
For we both know the secret of passion
is surrender to change that it brings.

I would dance for a time without knowing,
when my promise would have me released
For the flame that I am was born knowing
only grace lights the fire of peace.

POETIC LICENSE

Awakening from doubt I find
the truth a simple paradigm:
Surrender to the voice within,
transcendent be thy space in time.
No peace in clutching rituals
mundane their bittersweet rewards
Instead I choose a path that's sown
with dreams and paved with metaphors.

Harmonious exchange the flow
of rhythm at the speed of rhyme
Full-flavoured motion captured
by the shadow of a pantomime.
My soul receives the blessing of
a vision shared with heart and mind
As destiny reveals in One
more beauty than I'd hoped to find.

Not mine alone, this call demands
a sharing of all sacred fruit
For savoured first then planted
are the seedlings that shall take to root
A skipping stone may simply graze
the surface but with every touch
The ripple of an honest word
has power to accomplish much.

And so, I acorn, life the tree,
that would surrender all of me
A voice too small for arrogance
that nonetheless was meant to be.
Blind shaper of this liquid art
in-spired by a force above
Here offer up as humble fare
another flavoured breath of love.

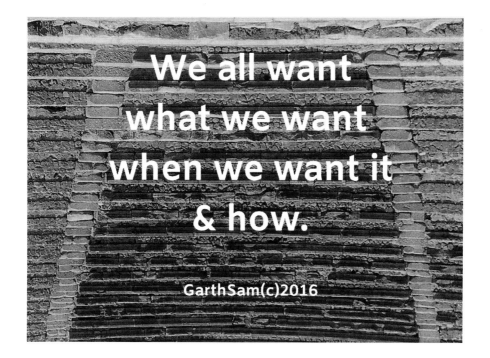

We all want
what we want
when we want it
& how.

GarthSam(c)2016

<u>*Encore!*</u>

How brilliant this feeling of mental expansion!

I savor and swirl on the tip of my mind

A delicate moment is frozen forever

And locked *holographic for memory to find*

Some years in the future when evening thoughts beckon

For vision restored to its glory-day best

I'll dine on the taste of this yesteryear blessing

And offer a toast from my heart to the rest!

The Castle and the Gate

Though some may claim the prophet's gift
to peer through time & space,
I'm no kin to Nostradamus
with sage knowledge of my fate.
Like the masses I am puppeted
by Destiny and Chance,
Whose capricious hands decide the grace
or chaos of my dance.
I can only pray like all men do
As life goes rushing by,
That the strings from which I dangle
Make me laugh more than I cry.
For around each cloudy corner
Behind which the future hides,
All my dreams may come to nothing
When desires are denied.
Or perhaps the whims will see me blessed
With days of love and joy,
so the man beholden to the beat
can still dance like a boy.
Fancy-free with light and wonder
Happy in his simple faith:
That each day's a magic castle,
And each morning is the gate.

Weapons of Mass Construction

From the rafters of righteousness to the seams of common sense,

the words are unexpected gifts to those who revel in change.

Shameless in dignity and balanced by faith, their message is borne

to defy stale emotions and chisel hopefully at jaded times.

Indomitable and impelled, mysterious and bright,

fantasy rolls across pain, erasing yesterday's shadow

with a force beyond myth and passion beyond desire:

a standard in love with itself,

forever searching for real meaning,

and as always

created

alone.

Day Won

Let us dance across quicksilver waves while our shadows play catch-up
For these are grace-full times of light & sweet promises
that wise men dare not deny.
The mischievous dawn beckons playfully
Ripe with an invitation to romp barefoot down primal pathways
Waltz through rose petal plains
Tickle toes on soft emerald lawnscapes
And frolic in sun-dimpled mud puddles.
Undaunted by the cosmic swing of seasons
We seize each peerless moment with gusto
Knowing that today is the only real dream to inhabit
And imagination is the breath behind life's greatest memories.
There is no vice of lost longing here to stifle our footsteps
Ours is not the strained soundtrack of nostalgia and melancholy
"Now" alone commands our attention with its perfect symphony
Boldly beating drums that inspire all seven senses
To celebrate the finest harmony of presence and essence.
Thus are we called to bravely make the most of our minutes
Until we reach the highest rung,
Until our songs have all been sung,
Until this fleeting dream is done
And one more shining day is won.

Echo's answer

The power of this conduit, so ultimately fair

Shall measure out in synergy, the truth that I lay bare

With words that cannot help, but share some secrets of the night

I know the stars conspire to add, their fire to my light.

I'll write a song of wisdom, woven with my very best

Inspired by immortality, I shall not fail the test

But rise instead and face the page, a wordsmith on the way

And offer ink in service to, the Muse I must obey.

Revel-ation

Let us share the wisdom & vision we claim
Though in fact we each know very little
For perhaps there are things yet to be seen
And some words that are still worth hearing.

The question is not whether keen ears exist
Nor minds that search for inspired images
But rather where & how many such seekers
Are eager to sip from the cup of muses.

For an instant the pieces are bound together
Plasmic soul-dust congealing into form
As we float in capsules of time & mind
Called to make the most of this dream life.

Put your best foot forward then & be counted
Express bravely what you discover to be true
It takes great courage to be well-known
For work that is honest, naked & free.

Thus exposed is the lot of each eager artist
Compelled to forge a way towards the inevitable
With authentic & eccentric revelations
They bare dreams for those who judge them.

Sunset

Plush violet skies expand
The heavens are anointed
Before darkness rules the day
Hope is dressed in golden robes.

At the end of the beginning
Shadows stake their rightful claim
A cool respite from bright viewpoints
Until fire rules the sky once again.

Journeys Here & There

Priceless

Great sages do *not* seek the spotlight
for they know that the flare of fame
only briefly illuminates the ego,
and true understanding has little to do with the fickle fancy
of either fans or followers.

In truth, all desire is a mirror for what is missing
and every shameless craving for celebrity
reveals first and foremost
the emptiness of a suffering soul
that prays to be filled with the love of strangers.

Still the world is most easily impressed
by the ambition of those who yearn to be heard
& crave to be seen
as if such hunger is a virtue
& need is proportionate to nobility.

Great sages know that the desperate pursuit of vain desires
Does *not* deserve more respect
Than the ultimate extinction of them:
And it is far better to live a contented dream life
Than to be unhappy chasing after an empty dream.

31

LifeSpeed

Once you accept the speed at which this life will pass you by
You may decide to spend more time pursuing how and why
For answers to bold questions are the steps that all must climb
And in this game odds favor those who seek to also find.

Though many are the roads ahead all journeys end as one
Each karmic tale of dreams and death is written in the sun
With open hearts to love some hear the siren song of Light
In counterpoint to those who heed dark whispers in the night.

No sooner said nor later done the deeds of man are seen
From naked steps to wherewithal and all points in between
The impact of each footprint shapes the moments yet to come
While history is written as the unrequited sum.

Thus choices make their peace with what the truth has left at stake
As wisdom proves that in-sight is the gift of Man awake
All flights of fancy crumble leaving Faith & Grace alone
To search within the eye of Time till Destiny is known.

Never forget
the power of play,.
for it is a joy-full heart
that inspires each truly
great leap of faith.

GarthSam(c)2015

Face to Grace

Embark on a journey
in search of a sunset
across many miles
on the path you would know.
Once in the center
of all that awaits you
dreams will take root
for your spirit to grow.

Follow the light in your eye
towards victory
much like the peace
men of faith call their own.
Blessed are those who find
diamonds of destiny
nestled in roots of
the seeds they have sown.

directions

The greater the burden, the wider the search
The longer the journey, the sweeter the church
The higher the mountain, the richer the climb
The further from righteous, the colder the crime

A glimpse of tomorrow, a page from the past
Each moment spills open, replacing the last
From dream to decision, from vision to goal
The best course of action, begins with control

For passion unbridled, has power to sway
From one to another, the state of the day
Whatever the channel, the promise remains
Devotion to purpose, shall register gain

Through causes ignoble, or those Heaven blessed
Free will is the challenge, and life is the test
All effort produces, that one constant state
Decisive in judgement, unstoppable Fate.

True & False

To seek & savor truth is the path to both grace & humility
But few have the courage to look closely at life.
The quest for real understanding must ultimately
Be the search for the essence of oneself
And that is a very challenging inner journey.
Like bittersweet gifts from the infamous fruit of knowledge
We cannot ignore the plight of mythical Pandora
For there are doors once opened that can never be closed.
From micro to macro & symbol to source
Everything is everything indeed
Related, connected & contiguous.
But for some the boons outweigh the burdens of insight
And the gift of wisdom is far more enticing than
The delusions of ignorance.

Sand Pages

In dire times I dream of peaceful waters

Adrift upon a sea of tender hope

The answers stir the dust of sacred quarters

And offer up salvation's gentle rope.

In spite of all the days that came before me

I realize tomorrow holds the key

So boldly I'll attempt a greater journey

With faith in grace to guide my destiny.

The Weight of Wanting

Everyone is born hungry,
Sucking desperately for life itself with each neonatal breath
And then for heartier sustenance still from breast or bottle.
As our cries mirror our simpler needs
One plaintive howl precedes another until satisfaction staunches sound.

Indeed, basic nature craves base fulfilment
No different from one species to the next on the lowest mortal tier
But rising wills & wants separate Man from beast
When the appetite for existence is complicated by the desire for more.

More than enough to ensure safe survival.
More than the perfect blessing of an unfettered breath.

We scrabble towards loftier goals & brighter things
With dreams whet by baubles someone else labeled precious.

So hard to resist symbols even without a conspiracy to co-opt
Our desire for something more tangible than life's fragile fiction.

Great ambition is celebrated as the most inspired call to action
And the price to be paid for a potful of gold.
From the motherlode of fools, to the mountain under Midas
we want it all but in the end, it is all just metal.

Time is the only legitimate currency with which we pay for our pieces
And rarely the favored coin we spend first on our peace.

CARPE

A moment is noticed as one bright transition
Relentlessly scrambles from promise to proof
Revealing the passion of all things made urgent,
By yearnings inspired most often in youth.

Each tremor of miracles flavored with promise
Providing the artist with fresh lumps of clay:
To shape-shift the eloquence of a new vision
All hands borne to action must first seize the day.

Still some will ignore Chance her wonder-full offers
And leave unrequited both romance & rhyme
Such souls will be branded regretful and wanting
For missing the clues to an auspicious time.

So challenge life bravely to grow beyond common
While cowards complain that the source was too deep
By chasing the river of love where it takes you
The bounty of poets will be yours to keep.

How to be One

Once upon a time
when I could only see the world
through the eyes of a child
I did not truly understand
that it was far more important
to choose how to live & who to be
than how to want & what to do.
I was taught to be "good"
but learned that obedience
was more celebrated than kindness
and competition won higher praise
than compassion.
Those who spoke loudest were heard
regardless of their messages
above the softer sounds of
both the sage and the seeker
for although many claimed to honor
the noble virtues of saints
I learned that most
did not follow their heroes
nor cast themselves as
humble heroes to be followed.

Instead they chased dollars not sense
fought for fortunes not freedom
ignored inhumanity as an inconvenience
and praised prosperity over charity.
In time I grew to wonder
why men settled for so much less
when they once seemed to know
that they could be so much more.

Then at last I understood:
we must each decide daily
whether or not to dispel the darkness
as beacons of hope
who illuminate & inspire:
For if with time
we are called to put away childish things
then s/he has matured well when
the Golden Rule is no longer a gilded metaphor
offered as guidance to children,
but rather the way & the walk
of all grace-full humans be-ing...
and having learned this precious lesson
I would do my utmost
to be one.

the etcher's anthem

there is a road to walk on, I will feel it 'neath my feet
as I travel in this body, with the characters I meet.

solo master of one journey, only pilot of this ship
self-important little presence, for the sands of time to strip.

but before I'm brittle bones, with no more substance to define
I will struggle up the mountain, that before me I must climb.

if it's written in the heavens, everyman must make his bed
I shall strive to gather wisdom, to secure my daily bread.

making more than less of each day, well before eternal night
knowing those who cherish sunrise, have more gratitude for light.

and as roots enjoy the sweet taste, of the early morning dew
So a Man must shake the tree of life, to savor all the fruit.

Heir & now

Steady grace is the dream that we yearn for,
even as Time always mocks such aspirations.

Nothing precious is ever fixed or unchanging:
neither love nor fortune remain constant.

The best of days too soon become a fragile pile of dust
and an evaporating puddle of memories

All borne away forever and for everyone
by a relentless stream of seconds.

But such is the irrefutable nature of things
so Men are wise to find joy in great moments

Those savory times when Fate is seemlessly
aligned with our humble interests.

It is then that bright crystal skies beckon
with panoramic promises of glory

And those who are determined to make their mark,
soar to heights unimagined by the less fortunate.

Voice out of Vacuum

These days have seen me write far less
than what the times have spoken
As though a moment felt and spent
is then a moment broken.

The source that shares the best of me
knows silence is a treasure
And yet I have an open need
to mark & mind & measure.

The glory of sweet innocence
that finds her way through danger
A noble deed of charity
committed by a stranger.

Both ruthless beasts that pose as men
But find delight in evil
And graceful saints who promise hope
is coming for the people.

I chart a course for wonderers
Who surf a sea of sunsets
To capture with my failing ink
the tastes of love & regret.

Those echoes & sharp images
That bind our hearts together
The days so bright & beautiful
we wish would last forever.

But few have means to freeze their dreams
Or scribes to save their stories
The unrecorded far outweigh
all deeds of grace & glory.

And so it seems I'm here to learn
Some words come to & through me
Like scars with nowhere else to go
I bear my sacred duty.

A pawn a-mused and bade to dance
a channel for the chore
And though at times I shirk the pen
I know I'll scribble more.

Shelter

and what if I were to rip you out of the cocoon
you have grown so fond of spinning
would you, I wonder, revere me or revile me
or would the shock of this bright emptiness
merely exaggerate your need for dark spaces?
true, the future stares back with selfish eyes
sharing nothing but lidded possibilities
but I enjoy a 360 degree view of the present
and what I see in it are the visions we could share if you let go
so tell me, where is it that you still find room to hide
better yet, given so many dynamic choices, why bother?
after all, an island is not the only shame-less shelter
and you are not a castaway.

The Long Familiar

In search of an African dream
I followed you here
so soon to discover that while
the sun remained the same
the face of your promise had changed.
Drawn & doubtful it bore the legacy
of heavy hopes.
I thought you knew but perhaps the years
had scaled your memory
chiseled down the details
humbled the more dangerous lines & motives
leaving only the ghostly
half-hearted whispers
of home.

Cause and Affect

Your soul is parched with thirst for greater goodness
To match so many nights you fought to know
The answers to both past and newborn footsteps
Chagrined, as you aspire to join the flow.

But have you not sent rays of hope into the darkness
And pierced the hood of doubt with words of trust?
For all the times surrender seemed an option
Your lead inspired further faith in us.

Anointed are the few who share their vision
Of ways and means to liberate the truth
Where effort finds its grace in hands of wisdom
Kind hearts are bound to touch the souls of youth.

Rewards are often naked without glory
The subtle gifts that whisper soft as dawn
As faith earns greater wealth from time than worry
Embrace the path that Fate has led you on.

Stoneflower Blues

With a sigh I stretch forward to claw at the night

Again & again it eludes my grasp

Indifferent to both torchlight & tenderness

The struggle is one-sided & of course I am alone.

Is there any doubt that these humble hands will fail to hold

That from which even the gods cannot exact a compromise?

I know the stealthy smirk of seconds

So confident & careless as they slither past my dreams.

Words & Needs

so many songs so much like these
with different words for different needs
but still of all of them I find
not one can change my state of mind
not one can change the way I feel
the life I lead the hardest deal
instead I'm bumped & pushed along
by every new amusing song
compose to make the dollars flow
to go where fashion only knows
a flash in one then out the next
soul-simple in a world complex
and yet if my pen spoke for all
no one would heed this cattle call
which means I champion those alone
who patronize the twilight zone
that queasy clan of men at work
those dreamers who in riddles lurk
behind their concepts deep in thought
indulging in their fertile lot
they sow the seeds of old desire
with secret thoughts of blood and fire

and dance along the edge of night
this way & that in headlong flight
from simple pleasures of the day
beyond the words too few can say
but wait they're not alone you see
they share that sacred path with me
in search of visions & a tune
bought dearly never born too soon
live rainbows reaching for the stars
eclipsing fear of pain and scars
and so I praise the opal skies
which opened this poor poet's eyes
and blessed me with eternal youth
the gift to those who search for truth.

Hurry no Hurry

Rush not towards anything good
As if you have the power to choose otherwise
For there is nothing truly good that lasts
And the sweetest taste once savored
Will also in time have the dry flavor of chalk.

Stall if you can in fact
Dig your heels into every minute
and grip seconds hard by your fingernails
Do whatever you can to imagine that you will stay
in that place
for even one moment longer
Because there is no moment
good or bad
that lasts longer than another.

We are all on the same rudderless cattleboat
Careening down a Nile of time
Bouncing off banks of days
& bumping off boulders of seconds
Until the fearless waterfall swallows us whole
And the dream gets the best of the dreamer.

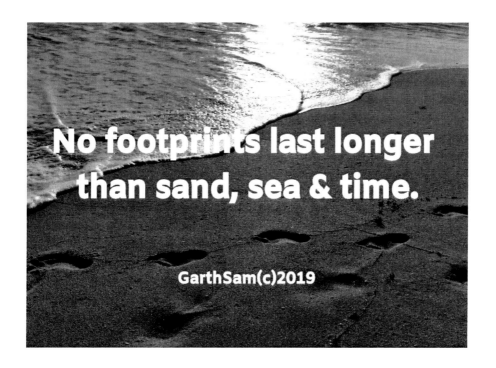

No footprints last longer than sand, sea & time.

GarthSam(c)2019

Peace of Purpose

I know now where the spirit rests,
upon the sleeping grass

That place too rich in metaphors
for dreaming hearts to pass

And if you choose to follow me
to where this beauty lies

Your life will not describe a tale
so rich in compromise

For "wants" are said to bring about
perdition's evil twin

Desire fat with emptiness,
and overstuffed with sin

Though hunger for a sweeter draught
means sorrow rules the day

True liberation has a price
that very few will pay

As Greed will write the sorry fate
of every desperate hand

Nirvana comes to those who build
their castles in the sand

And smile when these are washed away
as everything shall be

Reminding us that holding on
will never make you free

Instead to have that gentle peace
illuminate your soul

Surrender & seek inward first
to find your living goal.

From Bacchus to Bard

We are all junkies are we not?

each one of us addicted to our own
particular brand of sensation.

the narcotic we crave is the fulfillment of our passion

behind which second is never truly a respectable
position.

in this brave state of bliss I dare the world to deny me

for omniscience is my vine-ripened prerogative

and any brush with slippery nirvana requires an
awakening.

Time wields her devious devices

forever pulling on invisible puppet strings,

as yesterday's music is the reaper's theme song.

but still, there is a source of continuity in the poet's
voice

and madmen who joust with jesters or die for justice

always know where to find it.

Free Ways

in a world that's rife with carnage
I am mesmerized by beauty
here in contrast spread before me
for my senses to embrace
but the sweetest of these flavors
is the subtle taste of samadhi
with a whisper of the Voice
I hear a Symphony of grace

unencumbered by exposure
to the weight of future longing
I am pure again of heart
and rich with wonder's golden kiss
stepping lightly from the mud of dreams
that challenges my motives
I am free to soar on sacred wings
to claim a greater bliss

where I journey light is boundless
with the universe unveiling
both the elemental sunrise
and the transcendental dawn
thus attempts by night to bind me
to the darkness are impotent
for the chant of love immortal
is the song that guides me on.

The spin cycle

could it be we're all trapped in some way, shape or form
without comfort in transit, bruised battered & torn
into fragments of yearning for more of our selves
without which time is tasteless for whom toll the bells
as we spend precious hours attempting to dance
on a web-full of wonders & riddled with chance
in the hope for a fate written gently & fair
in a world rich with sorrow but still poor of care
where denial will cradle you shuddering wet
from this time to the next with a twist of regret
if you fail to assimilate what you must learn
lessons missed shall be waiting your next karmic turn.

Casting called

Tragedy, the eternal Greek
has a bittersweet flavour that compels my senses
and neutralizes my objections
for I love both heroes and martyrs
they die with such uncompromising character
And while a tiny voice wonders at the breadth of such
sacrifice
It does not speak loudly or long
For my focus remains fixed on that noble leap before
the dream-crushing bullet
with faith in purpose as cool comfort
when I visit the void.
Then may someone's memory of my shadow
be as vivid as my intentions
As resonant as my sacrifice
As indomitable as my spirit
And as sacred as my youth

Dreamcatcher

Where it comes from no one knows
but not for long before it goes
like all that has some life at all
beholden to the siren call
of seconds that must be the first
to make indifferent best or worst
like every breeze that's ever blown
or all the history that is known
and yet it need but strike a spark
to cast a light and crack the dark
this candle that is made of thought
forsaken and perhaps forgot
or sold to those without their own
who yearn for seeds they cannot sow
it claims a moment with its charm
like hope and faith keep all men warm
so would you know what thing is this
as powerful as Nature's kiss
forever felt but never seen
no more no less: a fleeting dream.

Iron Bridge

Across the many miles I've been
I seek to save the sights I've seen
By shadowing on naked page
Fresh images as yet to fade

But even with each word I write
I cannot capture day or night
The essence, yes, but not the truth
A taste of light but never youth

For though almighty pen I wield
The sands of time shall never yield
Their fallen fruits to taste again
Full-flavored feast served only then

One-time reward for fleeting dreams
The wisest counsel thus it seems
Is not to grasp for brittle past
In futile hope the hour will last

Nor pine for days no longer here
And memories forever dear
But rather to lock lips and know
Each sunset kiss we must let go.

Practice Pitch

When you allow your self to listen
You hear the sounds of confusion
A noisy distraction that many find amusing.
But behind the cacophony
Is an ocean of silence:
An infinite plane that beckons best
And all those who know peace
Live gently in the space
where the mind is still & quiet.

The Inspiration of Wonder

When stumbling past the cause of your confusion
And searching for the comfort of a goal
Explore the vivid contours of your passion
To soothe the restless aching of your soul

For boldly are we born to spin through moments
With reins of hope we try to tame the ride
Though often in our quest for joy & answers
The truth revealed sees many dreams denied.

The brave alone press on with faith undaunted
While humble hearts accept their sacred lot
When prophets offer peace instead of pleasure
Men suffer to be shown what they are not.

Thus all who choose the seeker's path must wonder
Why they were called to chase the setting sun
How lonely is the road that leads to wisdom
Until the way and why at last are one.

know - way - out

I was a man possessed
of many things, but learned of very little
And when I heard the loving song that called me forward
Indulgence stopped my ears
with the pleasure of familiar comforts
For I knew that the chosen are evermore and always
likewise the most challenged.

But a day arrived when
no solace was to be found
in either sweet adventures or sensuous nights
All glib pursuits lost their meaning,
and thus was I borne to my Destiny
A humble muse
swept aloft on the wings of wonder.

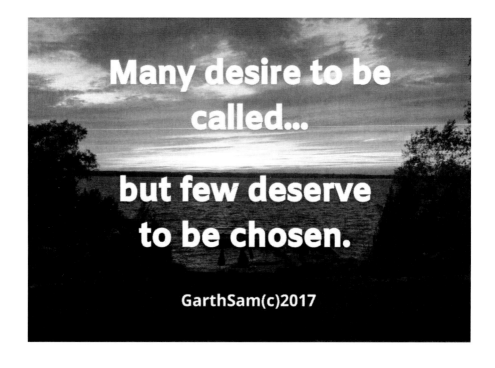

Choices

Would you care to peer through time for glimpses of tomorrow?
And if you knew your fate today what wisdom would you follow?
To make the most of who & what defines your way of be-ing
Where wills & wants compete for time before each fickle ending.

Old Ebenezer once was shown his present, past, & future
A phantom's chance to savor what a stitch in time might suture
But few are blessed with mystic guides who offer sacred counsel
Instead we fumble in the dark towards both known & novel.

A different dance one to the next, but same the peerless outcome
From single breath to elder's best, no moments can be undone
Forgotten men & icons both, too soon must run their life-race
As saints share death with sinners, so the reaper none can outpace.

Thus ask what moves you most towards your legacy or greatness
And if you knew the price of fame might you be happy nameless?
For want of naught does one enjoy the peace unknown to grinders
While vistas are the boon of those who hunger to climb higher.

Of taste and substance

As the ego is the mother of ambition,
so accomplishment is the child of desire.
For those who scale the greatest heights
are those who yearn the most to be there.
It is always a keen hunger for more that hones
the sharpest blades of conquerors & kings,
While men who are truly content
have no need for either edges or empires.

Thus begs the question that haunts so many
who live unsung lives between these poles:
Is the dream best fulfilled by an insatiable fire
or the gentle grace of peaceful waters?
And though there are as many sounds as options,
the answer remains selfishly the same:
To each their own destiny, and for all
but a moment in time to shine regardless.

<u>Non-Rocket Science</u>

Is there nothing fearless to be said in support of the Truth?

Not the differences of opinion between creeds and extremists

Just the simple understanding of the Golden Rule in action:

Namely, do unto others as you would have them do unto you.

Let us all ask a question that goes something like this:

Do they not see themselves and understand their deficits of design?

Or do they care so little about who they are that they do nothing?

Nature is extremely stubborn & set in her ways

So she alone is not to be blamed for bad behavior.

Character too is a chameleon in shades of forest and sea

Shapeless, formless & perfectly malleable

Thus shortcomings may be for lack of knowledge, skill, or understanding

But a Man must still be responsible for who he is
& the caliber of his conduct.

Haliburton Haiku

A lake of wet glass
Sees me looking at wisdom
Behind reflection.

A forest of leaves
Offers truth without speaking
In silent repose.

A moment lived once
Like breath in the winter sun
Has served its purpose.

Sun smiles in blue sky
Even when thunder crackles
And rain is waiting.

The stars are patient
Without effort they find peace
Is everywhere.

Dear Solace

Dear Solace,
I knew that I'd find your kiss here,
Far away from the lips of my pain.
Stir your precious draught for me
and settle my doubts
for your wisdom intimidates shame.

I have come to you dragging
My soul through the mud
Of confusion, that dullness of sight;
For I know as I stagger
Along this dark path
It is you who will show me the light.

What is broken shall mend
And the rancid grow fresh
With each breath of your fertile reply;
Subtle moments we spend
Will endear us as friends
Solace soothe me, for love never lies.

words from the well

An unscheduled stop
Once again,
At a place in the desert
Where your heart finds no comfort
In the knowledge of dunes.

The dryness is too familiar
And the space is too cold
You already know that breathing
Isn't the same as drinking
When you're thirsty.

So you look over your shoulder
Backwards to see forwards
Challenged by questions
Of both hours and dreams
That will not be forgotten

But neither yield the answer
Those playing fields are dark
To savor the sunshine divine
Life offers these words only:
Seek within, to be without.

Black Water

I have no fear of black water.
I have made peace with the opaque depths
This tiny bucket pours into the ocean
One breath at a time
Reclaimed by the brine
And as I surrender to the contiguous unknown
There are no cracks to fill.
No gaps between presence & essence.
Only the sum from which I was borne
A blind medium teeming with life
A liquid cavern of shadows that absorbs me
The ultimate aqua matrix.

I have no fear of black water
Though demons haunt the darkness
And monsters rule the seas at night
I too belong
As prey or soothseeker
This is a test I will pass or suffer
More intimately alone than apart
Every doubt dissolved
By faith and confidence

Every dream made meaningless
For I cannot write them now
I have swum too far out into the ink
And there are no terrestrial truths
For a Man to hold onto here
Only ebony tides
Patiently waiting for me to come home.

I have no fear of black water.
It is death incarnate
The void brought to life
Everything & nothing in perfect harmony
Is what happens when you swim at night
You let go & die
Only to be reborn
With birth as the first baptism
Every second can be a nocturnal float
As we return to the primordial womb
The richest of dark places
And emerge anew like the very first Man.

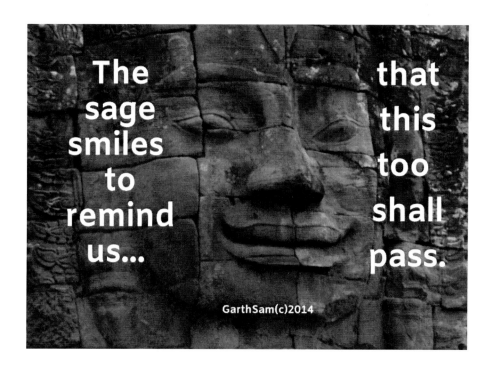

COAST of a CHANCE

This quiet breathes a soothing song

So much the match for times that bring me here

Away from the urban host,

Wet miles across those secret swells that favor
shores both lonely and inviting

They are no longer sacred, but in the darkness, I
shall lay fresh tracks

And share the weight I bear between the
footprints that I leave behind

Forever.

Worldly Ways
&
Outer Visions

say KNOW

This world shows little love for gentle softness
Fire & ice shape the powers that it breeds
Why then should I forsake my merry madness
While others laugh with gold in bloody sleeves?

You ask what many know is not the question
As if a stone was meant to float on air
Each judgement will reveal the final lesson
And all will earn their perfect karmic share.

But who shall deign to brand my deeds unholy
When my time to be seen has come and gone?
For wealth and fame protect me from my story
Indulgent in the selfish things I've done.

Was grace a state so ready to be conquered
That men were free to buy away their vice
A million camels would have passed through needles
Instead the wicked always pay the price.

Thus I am damned to suffer hell already
As penance for the evil spoils I've won
What point in changing modus operandi
Naught shattered can by willing be undone.

No doubt dark actions call for an atonement
And Time forgets what space cannot forgive
But less is more in terms of karmic burden
So sooner wise is better while we live.

Strength
without compassion
is the hallmark of brutal men
who etch their names
in the annals of history
by force & fear.

GarthSam(c)2017

beacheD blondE

She sits alone and loves the sunset
As the world goes sliding by
Thoughts of evening play within her
And she wonders with a sigh
If this day could last forever
Would it satisfy her dreams?
In the sanguine glow of twilight
All is not quite what it seems
Still the pulse that she remembers
Is a light she can't forget
And as memory offers comfort
Morning soothes the night's regret
So anointed she surrenders
To the bosom of her fate
Sea breeze kisses send her homeward
There for destiny to wait.

In Search of Mindspace

A journey through the halls of power
home of the infinite & the profound
reveals very little about the sacred workings of the mind
that mysterious net cast seductively across both planes
teasing conscious and unconscious lives
its impact belies its intentions, for control is critical
and belief is the key.
who knows why we turned to madness not ecstasy
that way seems to make so little sense & yet
even chaos can be friendly when familiar
both dreams & fears are born in desperate times.

Contra Diction

Our hearts break again as wicked men co-opt the weak and the desperate,
Beguiling some with false promises of honor and a noble purpose,
Manipulating others with both threats and rhetoric,
Bribing the disenfranchised to sell their scruples
And seducing the simple with the lure of fantasies fulfilled.

Ensuing atrocities leave us duly disgusted, our faith challenged
But we must remember that only a small segment of humanity has none:
The damned who suffer and seek corrupted company to share their misery
Do not and will never represent the majority.

They are a rare breed of barbarians who incite the murder of innocents
Those pitiless men decried by the bard as less than beasts.
We must remember that heinous deeds are the wont of very few
And such defective souls are as dark as they are disconnected.

For no one who truly honors the infinite Divine
Lives to wreak havoc on the parts that compose the whole.
Rather, all great masters of faith, spirit and wisdom
Regardless of nation, culture or creed,
Shine brightly as beacons of betterness because they see themselves in others
Intimately bound as members of but one human family.

With enlightened views and compassionate actions to match
They are the inspired antidote to malevolent propagandists
Whose ugly messages of hate compromise both conscience and comportment.
For though it remains sadly simple to recruit pawns for an evil agenda
We who live for peace and the elevation of our species
Are truly an indomitable force to be reckoned with.

United by our shared desire for harmony
Inspired by the language of light and the vernacular of hope
Our voices will always come together in a chorus of righteous indignation
And our song of universal love will forever ring triumphant
above the pathetic clatter of chaos.

Sparks in Glass Houses

Like broken birds that struggle on with nowhere left to go

the darkness of uncertainty hides cracks that will not show

behind the varnished secrets of the human capsule form

indulgent acquisitions hide the unimpressive norm.

As players deal their jokers dreaming time will never stop

nor lethal blade of Damocles find impetus to drop

those lost in selfish arrogance may not true villains make

but peace & love are oft the boon that greedy hearts forsake.

1, 2, 3 ... grow

1. What if you claimed the vast grace of this synergy
    Would you be brave enough to search and see?
    How you could dance on the edge of divinity
    Finding your faith in the truth you could be.

2. There is great proof in the teachings of avatars.
    There is pure light in the shadows of doubt.
    There is new faith in the way of detachment.
    There is still truth in the sound of a shout.

3. Trade in your Gucci for something more meaningful
    Treasure each sunrise far more than your car
    Search for the power within words of wisdom
    Mine for the riches that say who you are.

waves & ripples

You imagine what you do matters much & to many

That the pebbles you cast in the pond

Make greater waves than ripples

And your movements prove your life has meaning

But for every boulder hoisted & hurled

With a thunderous splash of pride

That ovation is only a fleeting whisper

No louder than a grain of sand falling

And no longer lasting than the humble moment

Marked by the same infinite hourglass.

This truth is the burden of both kings & slaves

The powerful as well as the penniless

For no one can carve their name in the River

Let alone dam its flow for an instant.

Ask even the Great to state their case in a millennia:

All eyes are closed & mouths are stopped with dust.

Ah but there is no comfort in such thoughts
When mortal fear is all that beckons from the shadows
Let us instead find cause to continue:
Substance in our labors & joy whenever possible
Let us chase boldly after
Purpose & promise until we are ready to surrender.
A dream perhaps, a reason for being
A mountain to climb or an empire to build
Some mark to make against all odds
For the fortunate few who can pause before passing
To reflect with humility
On the laurels of a life well-lived before lost.

Picture Perfect

What's **wrong** with this picture I ask, and the answer is punctuated with
gunfire.

Two men, arms linked, well-fed, are smiling into the eyes of the world.

This is not Aleppo with its ripe, pillaged memories.

Flash-frozen is an image of another, safer, colder place,
where fresh cigar smoke and sherry are signs of moral anesthesia.

Those who stagger in front of the camera here are drunk and/or blind,
but **they** are not bleeding.

Because this is not Aleppo.

That land, rich with pain and terror, is far, far away.

Who cares when the scythe severs another timeline, ending another
relationship, closing another door.

Wide-eyed and breathless: nothing makes much sense there apart from
the screams.

The screams, curses, prayers and weeping: certainly **not** smiles.

Not in Aleppo.

But **they** are smiling in the picture, just like old school chums, as if they
don't know anything about it.

As if it were just another day. As if they really played no part. As if.

A mother cries, a baby dies, a leader lies, a poet sighs...for Syria.

Pity the wicked
for they are always
sad, scared
&
lonely.

GarthSam (c) 2019

p.i.p squeak

* peons in power *

They make me sad these petty little people
Stuffed into their roles like silly proud sausages
How they indulge each opportunity to feel significant
All puffed up with smug illusions of authority.

I do not envy 'pips' their attachment
to holographic empires
Bought, sold & traded as easily as they are
But I understand the cog's hunger for greater meaning:
We all want to believe that we really matter.

Were it easier to exchange need for know-how
and worldly wealth for wisdom
Many more would find the substance they crave
Without disrespect for both others and their karma
Real men would roar
and leave little mice alone to squeak.

all in

To the modest mite every dragonfly is a magnificent beast
Darting fearlessly through the skies on whirling wings
An apparent master of the heavens & beholden to none
But contrasting perspectives make all the difference

For even the largest living creature is limited
by the scope and scale of its focus, understanding & beliefs
Such that the mite's impossible hero is dwarfed by its mythical namesake
As the peerless dragon too is immediately eclipsed by the sun.

And yet the kernel contains the corn,
as each thought is a seed of the omniverse
Chiseled fragments no larger than a grain of sand
are nonetheless essential to the Whole
Every bit playing its humble part as an integral puzzle piece
Without which nothing could be the same nor the circle complete.

Thus Time may collude with the illusion of dramatic distinctions
But from one moment to the next neither mite nor man is irrelevant
Everything is everything as the dragonfly becomes the dragon
And from the mind of either, the mite's world is dreamed into be-ing.

MEA SURE.

Not for purchase nor for hire;
Its mettle survives the test of both acid and fire.
Uncorrupted by the gnawing efforts of one,
And uncompromised by the molten passion of the other:
This virtue stands defiant in spite of temptation's bravado,
That presumptuous barrage, so keen, so timeless,
Sly leveler of both giants and geniuses,
Monarchs and madmen, peasants and priests alike,
All fickle farmers of unripe promises.
But not Honor, a shining crown unblemished,
Inviolate, indomitable, & invaluable.

Honor,
as mighty as faith, as perfect as love,
As sacred as truth, a venerable treasure wisely guarded,
Available to all but embraced by too few.
With reverence we salute you,
And the hearts of real champions swell to sing your praises.
Hail Honor, brave Honor!
Hallowed be thy fame, and noble be thy name.

Not *JUST* work

Enticed by the promise of daydream's tomorrow
We celebrate numbers excited when we grow
Our gardens of currency, fruits of spent labor
As days become balance sheets, cash is the flavor
Of saccharin moments, devoid of nutrition
And lacking the substance once found in religion
Our joy becomes tricky to find time to pay for
In spite of the fact we work harder to ensure
The gold in our coffers protects us from yearning
For treasures of wisdom and sources of learning
While sages mine deeply for truth over profit
All avatars prove that it isn't "where" we sit
But "how" that determines the wealth we may own
And the harvest most valued from energy sown
To enrich other lives with benevolent purpose
Golden moments created are gracefully priceless
For though dollars and sense are what many men miss
Those who work to spread love earn the best hope for bliss.

Price-point

Captivated by consumption
Distracted by the quest for finer things
So many wander through their days
Indifferent to the plight of the needy
Committed first to stuffing their faces
Filling their closets,
and polishing their purchases
they find little time for compassionate deeds
or divine duties
and imagine themselves safe in their sweet satiety
while others starve for lack of mere pennies.
What then is truly bought and sold
When superfluous acquisitions,
banal baubles,
and trite trinkets
are paid for with spiritual currency?

The accumulation of great
material wealth is proof of
neither genius
nor goodness...
but it does say a lot about a
person's values, needs &
priorities.

GarthSam(c)2019

50c or a dime

Today I met a man who committed no crime
all he wanted from me was 50 cents or a dime
I denied all good conscience, fought my guilt tooth & nail
lacking foresight to know in the end I would fail
for its failure I feel as I think of him now
because I could have helped him, in some way somehow
"50 cents or a dime Sir is all that I need.
I may die all alone but it won't be from greed"
still I held fast my change & he soon let me be
shuffling off down the street to repeat his sad plea
now I'm left writing this, feeling weary & small
knowing one struggling man thinks I don't care at all.

phoenix read

Ahhh.
So much conveyed by so little,
And yet subtlety moves in the same direction
as trauma:
For all truth waits only to be seen
by patient eyes.
I looked & saw the fire that has ironed the surface
Of a soul-wrinkled brow,
Smooth;
but the heat has left an impression,
indelible etchings, imperfectly seared.
There.
Dull reminders of a girl who staggered under
the weight of her
Confusion, seclusion, illusion,
And was bent but not broken:
A testament to the supple grace of youth,
Which yields & therefore endures.
Swaying, weaving, shining, screaming, she stands:
Mythic, defiant, flying in the face of destiny,
Laughing at the sound of terror,
dancing on the edge of panic,
until time exhales,
its breath a singular promise,
the herald of change,
the voice of evolution,
expansive & expanding,
thus a woman is borne to higher ground.
<u>You.</u>

No Foolin'

The biggest buffoons are not jesters or clowns
who amuse with expressions & antics,

Far more troubling are those who believe they possess
greater wisdom than masters & mystics.

Whereas seekers of truth place humility first
having learned pride makes folly a blessing,

Little souls with big egos are wont to imagine
they are privy to what Life is thinking.

But for every bright veil from the Mystery lifted
are a thousand & one further facets,

And a poor man is he who presumes to have caught
all the ways of the world in his basket.

So don't suffer with gladness the hubris more common
than sense to the ignorant many

For like pearls before pigs are not truffles to dig
Only fools trade a pound for a penny.

To yoke

I am neither the sound nor the sensation that is born when I bend
I am simply a sagging bodysuit that cries to be rigid
But longs to be loose
My crooked spine is a reminder to be humble
Because no matter how robust I imagine myself to be
I am bent & broken by nature
Just a petrifying clump of salt, sins & sentience
More brittle by the second
With only the promise of stone sans sense
Waiting indifferently ahead
Despite best efforts by most to deny the inevitable
I cannot be so foolish or desperate to believe in forever
That word has no meaning for the who I call me
Although many find far greater comfort in the dream of immortality
Never pharaoh nor king who paid the world to live forever did
All men once called "Great" and others still called "god"
Are now nothing more than forgotten wisps of ash & dust
Tiny fragments of no interest except to a handful of historians
Ego made zero by Time & power proven pointless
All ambition almost instantly irrelevant
Except for each moment of be-ing
But that is enough for the illusion of meaning & the birth of desire
For we were made to cling,
To crawl, cherish, chase & conquer
Inspired by intellect & motivated by fear
Faith offers the sweetest comfort when thoughts explore the future
Because there is no peace without purpose
And we all need something to believe in until we don't.

The Scales of Life

The devil's deal is ever real
As much a truth as guns or steel
But think it not a tale that's told
By Lucifer when souls are sold
No magic scripts the balanced dance
That some call Fate & others chance
Instead for every choice a price
Paid both in virtue & in vice
To match the potency of dreams
Ambition costs more than it seems
And thus the truth: for every side
The opposite we must abide.

Main & Broken

she stumbles onto the bus in a confusion of unfinished dreams

torn and weary her spirit staggers as she drags it along

I mark the glances,

check the stares,

note the indifference,

and wonder if her sisters are crying

or why not.

this little girl has lost her way home, and if hope has an address

she's lost that too.

she doesn't sit down though free seats beckon blindly:

perhaps she has learned not to believe in the promise of empty
spaces.

a bell tolls, a light flashes, and time enforces its grip on our
journey.

The back door coughs open, regurgitating its shaky cargo,

and as she steps into the purple twilight

I can almost hear the sound of fresh bruises.

Q or A

It is rarely new questions that men seek

Rather, most hunger for time-tested answers

In a world with so many unfathomable dimensions

Heavy hearts & busy minds have little interest in further obscurity

There aren't enough explanations as it stands

Just a curious collection of irresistible moments

Gushing by without pause in an evaporating cascade of possibilities.

As every disaster leaves us wondering how & why no one is innocent

So too good fortune is both a sweet & mysterious muse

We do not know if anyone is out there listening to our prayers

Nor do we have the language to command luck

Life happens & we play our parts bravely

Imagining at most points that our desires really matter

& our efforts mean something bold.

But ultimately it is all revealed as a whisper in the wind

Not as loud as a shadow nor as large as a teardrop

We crawl, run, dance, trudge & stagger

Towards the same unavoidable wall

Impossible to scale or even peek past

It looms indifferent to both fear & faith,

As neither can stop the end of mortal days.

Still we fight hardest to stay upright & breathing
Cling desperately to the cliff for as long as possible
Until at last it becomes clear there was only ever one question
That all men were born to eventually ask
But no one ever lives long enough to answer it.

Honors Worth

How much is your dear honor worth? Believe me mines expensive.

And those who sell their scruples cheap, make this Man apprehensive

I'm not saying you're a member of that lower moral class

I'm just asking if we're dealing here with diamonds or with glass.

Are you honest with your business or is slick the rule of thumb?

After all it's no one's fault if some are quick and others dumb

So it goes with human nature, minus claims of wrong or right

Mister Gray has culled the very best, of all things black and white.

Only God knows whether choices are the measure of a man

And besides, what's good or badness if it's all part of the Plan?

Still for those who seek to live the noble meaning of divine

True integrity is priceless and defies the wrath of time.

LOVE'S LABORS LOST

The forgotten soul is delivered on a paper plate

With time purchased, a life is slowly spent

As kaleidoscopic dreams are diluted by daily distance.

That hungry space between what was once and the present

is drained of young longing but thick with regret.

Each fishhook moment swallowed

in the name of another man's dream,

adds disappointed fragments of mediocrity

to the weight of an insidious necklace

Remember then this:

once co-opted,

an uninspired alliance is the price of blunted passion.

a paper product

a paper product that I can burn & easily commit to the atmosphere
compels me to quarter stretched limbs & defeat all comers
it dare not challenge the sun but on this world it controls night & day
and can shatter the darkness
oh yes this conceited little rectangle has done so many times
provoking the flames that would happily consume it
a vulnerable force indeed but seductive nonetheless
carved from corpses this fragile monster of mashed flesh
is no longer organic yet still it grows
spreading like a pestilence
devouring souls & co-opting hearts
indifferent & absolved of any remorse
it's just paper as we all know,
but it holds sway over life on earth & can buy my last breath
secure in the knowledge that might defines right
an unstoppable cliché this streamlined product
filthy with the touch of greedy hands
who can say where they've been or what they've done
infected with paper power
I can't beat it although I might still try
what a vain little morsel I'll make when it sets its chops on me
but don't worry:
I'll put up a fight & with any luck who knows?
I may even manage to get stuck in its teeth.

soul chalice

This tender temple, nature's gift

a sole reminder of the rift

between the chalice and the whole

though sweet reunion spells the goal

As sanguine aspects cleave to bone

together all must walk alone

borne on through Life's relentless race

till future sands of time erase

keen musings, myths and metaphors

those dreams that come and go before

we offer up one final star:

the legacy of who we are.

First Borne

Borne on soft leather & sacred drumbeats
I whirl and I wonder
Do they see me behind those countless eyes?
Here, far below the gleaming sky castles
I am a hungry memory dancing on broken grass
That once breathed the name of another.

S/he could not comprehend the skyscraping steel bones
That surround this humble oasis now
For it is only a puddle & not a great lake
A fragile flower, not an endless forest
So I must try to make peace with the ghosts
Even as I fight to cast a brave new shadow.

This is not over and we are not done
I want to scream at the blank panes
To shatter them all & leave the gaping wounds naked
Like I am behind my timeless regalia
Stripped of the present
They will have even less claim to the past.

We sing to remember but I dance to forget.
The impossible towers of victory that surround us
Look down with confident curiosity
Possibly amused but no longer afraid
Of sun-kissed savages & humble heathens
With their souls in the mud.

But still we stitch buckskin & match feathers
As tribesmen united in defeat
All bands singing songs of survival
We gather to grow beyond the sounds of lamentation
And to remind the watchers
That we yet know who we are.

Yes, our blood feeds the land & our tears fill the lakes
But our feet will never stop dancing
No matter how small the circle
It contains the eternal heartbeat of our ancestors
And those who cannot see me
Must nonetheless know forever that we were
First.

Ear Ways

No man speaks for all men.

Neither the greatest of saints nor the wickedest of sinners

can capture the attention of every ear.

History proves that even the most celebrated souls

whose words flow with benign grace

from the spring of Universal Love

are ignored by those who prefer

power over piety

treachery over truth

and greed over goodness.

Some segment of humanity hears every message

as diverse desires define one's draught of choice:

thus expressions of both harmony and hatred

find dedicated listeners

who reflect and respond accordingly.

But while the wise that heed the former

are ever-blessed for their benevolent ways

the hateful,

the cruel,

the selfish

and the corrupt

who cannot hear and will not listen

always,

suffer.

the weight C carries

What bandage mends, what poultice heals
The wound to soul, a mother feels
When not for all maternal might
Can she who bore child, win the fight
Against the Reaper, grim and cold
Who on her babe, lays strangle hold
Impassive and unmoved by screams
Against a random fate that seems
Impossible, and heinous too
Yet hopeless if indeed it's true
That breath shall never more delight
The frame once suckled through the night.

Thus torn from self, the living rain
All words of comfort, heard in vain
For none can fill the empty space
Nor conjure up that state of grace
When safe between the loving breast
Dear future lay in peace to rest
Untroubled by the vice of man
Tomorrow's joy, the only plan
As solace claims a foreign name
While ravens cry seems full of blame
Upon the overburdened heart
Of one whose best still failed the part
Or so alas, she may believe
Till time and prayer, grant their reprieve
And usher in the soothing truth
That Heaven's best is saved for youth.

Uncalled

it is sad to see a lonely man
surrounded by millions
but locked in solitude
cut off & adrift
at night he cries.

it is sad to see a lonely man
knowing the balm to soothe his pain
lies just outside his tired reach
a brief moment away
but a world apart.

it is sad to see a lonely man
all pride and poison
wax & steel
imprisoned by careless years
that cannot forgive their quarry.

it is sad because a man alone
has neither brotherhood nor home
and thus must face each frozen day
with empty hopes the night will stay.

sorrow

no value to measure this leaden grief
its numbing weight could crush a thousand souls
the memory of you yields no relief
a stealthy poison still takes its toll.

laid bare at last I learn the bitter truth
no eagle ever dared to touch the sun
and sadly too I saw your golden youth
was ruined well-before its time had come.

Heroes

To whom shall we turn for comfort when our heroes are gone
For Death does not discriminate between inspiring icons
& those far sooner forgotten for less
No one is immortal in fact,
Only in the fickle record of great legacies well-preserved
Once in stone, twice in stories & now in the annals of e-mages.
We may blaze for a moment with brilliance or flicker unrequited,
But both good & bad men die young
Destroyed by chance or choice
As neither fame nor fortune grants favor with the reaper
And sometimes celebrity sharpens the scythe that much sooner.
Still, even giants who survive to be ancient
Those indomitable figures most revered & resolute
Eventually leave us to process their passing
Shriveled by time, exhausted by expectations & humbled by truth
At last they too exhale one final breath
In spite of prayers & protestations
No amount of gratitude is enough to save them or ourselves.
The wheel turns & farewell is forever so we must press on.
United by shared losses & memories
Empowered/inspired by the deeds of the dead to imagine better days
Sadness gives way to solace when we realize in the end
That our heroes did not live to be idolized or mourned
On a pedestal or pyre
But rather to surrender fully to their fate
To do what they were called to do regardless
And by so be-ing exceptional
Show us that the greatest gift from lost heroes
Is a reminder to live bravely on purpose
So that one day as we share & shine
Via art or inspired impact
We too light the way for others.

The Art of Love
&
Lust

Under-taken

How I long to be stolen.
Taken away from conventional company
By a force beyond resistance.
Made captive as both the student & the slave
Blissfully bound by ecstatic cables of yearning.

Chain me to the ethereal divine with moonbeams
And cage my consciousness with rose petals.
The sweetest draught of true freedom
Requires the deepest breath of surrender
So let me inhale it completely & be done.

Yes, how I long to be stolen.
Held choiceless & therefore innocent.
Beholden to the grace of an omniversal truth
That has me sing without censure
Indomitable, doubtless & inspired.

If there is a pure way in let me earn it
through the dissolution of my fruitless edges.
Call me. Claim me. Conquer me.
I would yield with the reverence of a paladin
to be swallowed whole by a perfect love.

in Sync

The night has penned us a love melody

Oh so perfect and soulfully pure

That if it were played by a symphony

Our sweet sounds would make music seem poor.

Deeper and wider than lightyears away

So much stronger than infinite time

Soft as the morning sun's gentle caress

Is the bliss of our spirits in rhyme.

The Ocean in a Wineglass

Twin diamonds light a fire in the moments when I think of you

Inspired by my desire are the promises we spoke for two

Adrift in the beginning when the joy of love was summer-fresh

I rediscovered music in the rhythm of your graceful flesh.

Now lavender & jasmine yearn to boast the fragrance of your breath

While dew-enchanted willows lack the softness of your satin breast

Beyond the sweetest sound you sing a melody of light & lace

And cradled in your eyes I see the beauty of an angel's face.

So many are the epithets a man could write in praise of you

The rainbow's fabled treasure pot could only hold a tender few

Like effervescent nuggets shining sacred in the summer sun

Pure golden are the moments in your arms that I alone have won.

And thus should any dare to vie for that which I have found in you

Their hapless aspirations would affirm this omnipotent truth:

The wealth we share as lovers renders moot the crown of every king

For you my Queen are rich enough, to teach the very birds to sing

Everything is as important
as the time
that you commit to it...
& everyone *feels* as important
as the time that you
share with them.

GarthSam(c)2019

Yes know

Yes know
this space is nothing more
than the dreams floating between us
in bright bubble bursts of pure possibility
each moment a sacred stage
for our love dance
across borders, miles & motives.

Yes know
we were bound to share everything precious
as deeply as Siamese hearts
too grateful to be distracted by memories
for these are the very best of days
when presence defines our purpose
and we are blessed with
the bounty of now.

Smoke & Mirrors

Like the taste of hope on the lips of a condemned man

Your essence promises sweet relief & infinite possibilities

If only I trade shadows for the light that tames darkness:

I'd be a fool to overlook a gift that could heal the rift.

So my faith throws feckless fear & ego into the void:

The foggy dreamscape parts, the curtain lifts, & the veil drops.

Doubts are diminished as illusion gives way to illumination

Making clear that nothing is more natural & less magical than

You.

Reflowered

In a room without petals
Life is missing its scent
As if payment for fragrance
Has already been spent

In a room without petals
Every color seems wrong
Amidst charcoal and taupe
Rainbows do not belong

In a room without petals
All the walls too are bare
So the art that you see
Has no sizzle or flare

In a room without petals
Time is never your friend
He will seek other playmates
To both tickle & bend

In a room without petals
It is hard to remember
Both the flavors of morning
And the taste of September

In a room without petals
Every dance is a dirge
With a sad somber tempo
That the mind's ear would purge

In a room without petals
There is no soothing grace
Just the heartbroken sigh
Of a voice lost in space

In a room without petals
Even laughter sounds wrong
Like whenever a singer
Forgets words to a song.

In a room without petals
There is nothing to say
Until Love fills the void
And Her light shows the way.

Yearn In

Yearn towards me
stretch your instincts & stroke my longing
with wet whispers & wanton fingers
there, in that sacred space where time retreats
search & you will find our molten love
carved from cravings for sweet sensual release
my body is oiled & open to your touch
the muse with orchid lips proclaims our freedom saying
these are ripe times for daring dancers
so together I am ready to play without thinking
and surrender to all manner of bold pleasures.

Yearn towards me
with a willing mouth & a wild tongue
for my taste is hot kisses that match passion to poetry
as above so below, make it twice the hard way in
till I cannot breathe for want of even deeper synergy
but still beg to feel the heat of your hands upon me
a grateful hostage to sensation
and when the dawn spreads her dewy petals
inviting us to the humid hearth of an erotic celebration
take me moaning on a hilltop at sunrise
knowing this delicious dreamscene
will never come again.

O

Never peace without purpose, nor love without trust

All great passion is written by instinct and lust

From both wicked indulgence to sensuous grace

So our pleasure finds meaning when time is erased.

As the moment is lost & the sacred is found

There is nothing to which "you" & "I" remain bound

But the joy of forsaking our selves to the dance

In the throes of surrender to time and to chance

Going inward and outward together as one

Consummation of purpose sees symmetry won

Till we climax transcendent with luminous gaze

Giving thanks for the gift of such wonder-full days.

CLICK

I wandered & waited,
Beholden to the pulse of destiny
As are we all
Searching to find a rainbow in a snowstorm
Always hoping that within the falling flakes
A light would appear
There
Inspired too by a quest
She would answer the call
With a smile for my eyes alone.

A thousand and one nights unbroken
Then more
my breath withheld
And my soul untamed
I walked alone & knew not how my name felt
Until it tasted your lips.

Then static became silence
As grace emerged from the din
A crescendo of form & substance
Dressed in fantasy fare
With ribbons of sunshine & moonlight brocade
Love stepped on stage
And I found you.

My siren Calypso
Borne on e-waves across the distance
Freedom's truth is simply our submission
To the space where all is No-Thing
Minus egos & edges
Being close is much deeper than a name.

Now these dreams play songs of longing
For I know the dance was won
By the daughter of twin rainbows
And the winter's favorite son.

Gifted

I looked within for truth and found
your image framed with light and sound
as if from heaven did descend
an angel called to put an end

To queries you and I once shared
about with whom we would be paired
not merely for a kiss or two
or lonely nights as many do

But rather for a time profound
as souls both intertwined and bound
to hold the lover's torch aloft
and laugh where injured hearts would scoff

At dreams of two becoming one
divinely blessed beneath the sun
we shining dancers rich in faith
so grateful for this time and space

For you see me and I see you
with eyes that know the quest is through
and thus we praise the One above
for giving us this gift of love.

The Shadow's Smile

in dreams

alone

i tread

where none would choose to go:

a hostage

of my subconscious

a prisoner of the dark hours.

through deserts wet with blood

and torn by strife

i am haunted by the night

and find no comfort there.

still,

without the whirlwind there is peace.

a gentle breeze,

a tender touch,

a finger's breadth away is you.

the shadows smile as our hearts meet

and all is healed by love.

Liquid Whispers

Share with me chica, a sweet breath of moments
With time shining brightly as we two play one;
Let's gather together a dream and a reason
To leave far behind what cannot be undone.

Our paths have converged here on one sun-soaked island
Through Liquid's bold rhythms were we bade to come;
And wherein the way shall forever be written
This language is overstood only by some.

That bold group who see life for all of its blessings
And drink with a passion from deep in the well;
We'll join them and dance freely from the beginning
No mind for a future that no man can tell.

So challenge the notion that dreams live forever
Tonight it was magic that spoke through our lips;
And although the rising sun must claim tomorrow
Perhaps dawn itself will soon envy our kiss.

In Praise of Euphoria

Come join me in a sea of bliss

Sweet wind-borne captive of my kiss

As we transcend both space and time

My hand in yours, your heart in mine

Beholden to the cosmic chance

That bade us share this autumn dance

Though strangers once we may have been

All unions are not what they seem.

For those who were, are meant to be

Entwined again, most naturally

Until the magic that they feel

Reveals to all their love is real

Soul-crafted in the dream for two

Now savored both by me & you.

The Dragon & the Genie

The vessel is yours but the talons are mine
As caress writes a summons to share the divine.
For so many years captive, awaiting the key
Now the touch of a dragon has set your soul free.
Fellow ancient, I sky-rider, from distant land
On a quest for Time's wisdom, found you in the sand.
Humble chalice, but Fate shines as bright as the sun
To reveal without censure, what our karma has won.
Yours, the spirit of fantasy, caught in a trap
Mine, the power of ecstasy, there to unwrap.
Thus I ask golden genie, to yield this unto me
Every emperor's dream of his wishes times three.
May the heavens almighty so honor my voice
As I lay claim to wonder with each magic choice.
First, I wish without compromise, no more no less
That you find peace and purpose, for true happiness.
Next, I ask of what powers may reign up above
That your heart shall be filled with the glory of love.
And enfin, I request with my third and last wish
That my lips hold forever, the taste of your kiss.
These three things I plead for in Venus' name
If undone, rest assured; I would wish them again.

L-emental Segue

I too am a seeker of love's tender graces
Like you in my search for that magical bliss
But far stands between hopes of one and another
In finding their way from a dream to a kiss.

Cold oceans of compromise, seas wet with mannequins
Posing as more than mere figments of truth
The depth of desire for soul-sanctioned resonance
Challenges many to hunger for youth.

A time ripe with feelings of hope for the moment
Twin lives intertwined as a lock greets her key:
We long for the taste of immaculate union
And pray that our hearts once again will be free.

But never is when pushing hands shall encounter
Those moments gray karma alone must inspire
For only when love strikes the match of our senses
May heaven's reward fan that exquisite fire.

AQUA VIVA

Clear was the water you offered to comfort me
Pure was the spring that it came from
Sweet was your gentle reminder that harmony
Flows from a source truly wholesome.

You bade me swallow your gift with rare tenderness
Simply committed to quenching my thirst
I who am challenged to always replenish
The well that I use to fill other cups first.

Thus do I count myself blessed & rewarded
So precious are sips from a soul such as yours
Faith resurrected by love's perfect ladle
I give thanks again for the grace that it pours.

Lost and Found

I tried once to give you
An ocean of petals
And offered myself as your island

Scaled the arch of a rainbow
In search of an answer
To brave questions beyond my command

Then my nature did guide me
Above all the trappings
of both science and duty to state

Till at last I arrived
On the breath of a prayer
At the promise of spring by your gate

There I watched as the seed
You had sown long before
Mirrored time in its quest to unfold

As you opened your door
To a stranger no more
And stepped in to unfetter my soul

In your garden I found
Both the light and the sound
Of far more than a passionate scene

For with love so divine
Blessing your lips and mine
We discovered the taste of a dream.

Once Upon a Midnight Mist

the night's embrace
with a touch as generous as fantasy
is calling out for wet lines
where moist planes intersect
in a world of pleasure and lace:
would you meet me there?

my essence extended
reveals a linear strength
seeking both sunlight and shadows
bold appetites yearn to find
an intimate sensual space:
would you meet me there?

this dream manifested
begs a molten reply
to the summons once bidden
there is no passing by
on the cusp of each moment
on the edge of all sound
stands a vision transcendent
where surrender is found.

CLOSE

the space between, an anxious gap - slight yet overflowing with anticipation - surrenders at last to the tempest - borne via molten sculpture - forming art repossessed - instinct alive between the humid pockets of flesh and fabric - repressed then relieved as explorations intensify - yielding voracious wants too great to reconsider - what needs must have dominion over

and then there is nowhere left to go save inward - along converging planes - until the apex offers a destination one deeper - relieved of all friction - there outside finds home within - a warm and welcoming hearth - so seamless the connection defies separation - as two grow together in rhythm - perfect moments evaporate with steamy breath - a vaporous signature - the herald of love's peerless combustion - declaring the height of the feast.

Full Circle

Anointed though we are in truth, one cannot help but wonder

At the grace divine that brought us here, and so I'm left to ponder

Were a breath withheld, a word unsaid,
would Fate have seen us follow

Other visions, dreams and pathways, to a different tomorrow?

Or was this enchanted journey, ever written in the sand

Carved on arrows fired by Cupid, ever-promised, ever planned

That the day would dawn when you and I,
would share each sunrise breath

Bless the glory sung between us, and swear unity till death.

My commitment stands almighty, forged with tenderness and faith

For within my heart there is for you alone a sacred place

Where the best that I can offer, I will always give to you

And before the Holy witness, I proclaim this love is true.

So perhaps we might have turned, a different corner on that day

When the stars aligned with smiling eyes, to see us on our way

But no edges could deter us, from the perfect whole we seek

For our souls were meant to join as one: a circle now complete.

Cloud Song

Tonight the rain dances on my window.
I know you like the sound
so my heart aches towards you.
Across the miles I stretch with a message of love & longing.
The distance magnifies my feelings
swelling memories & filling in those familiar wrinkles.
No better than the joy of earlier days
when we knew only our very best.
Can you sense me here in the dark?
My chest dreams of being your pillow
and desire sings as the rain drums a wet rhythm.
With you I dare to wax romantic again
like I've never really forgotten that voice,
so listen closely & you will hear it.
After all, that's what you do best

Every molten moment
is the forge
for fools,
saints & sinners
alike.

GarthSam(c)2013

Eros exposed

That special blending and bonding of bodies
Free from the mundane concerns of modesty
Liberated from distractions by desire
Purposefully directed towards simple pleasures instead
Profound interactions that promise the deep satisfaction
Enjoyed by sensuous seekers and indulgent adventurers
Who tickle Passion's muse with mischievous feathers
Just to see her lips part with breathy sighs
And notorious love smiles
Honestly revealed without self-censure
Amorous limbs are spread & stroked
Teased and tantalized in homage to the just bearable
lightness of being
Sensation is written along every inch of every moment
An oasis of possibility beckons over each languid curve
And within every valley
A river of fantasy flows into a dream of erotic combustion.

Bouquet

I sought to carve a marble memory from the ether of great moments
Knowing still that Time evades the most desperate efforts to hold her
Like a fool who tries to stop the tide from swallowing sand and footprints
My will was fixed to attempt the impossible.

The seasons mocked me with cruel heat and harsh tears of rain
Nature spread death in my wake as mountains quickly crumbled
No vain hope prevailed against the eternal endgame
And thus I stood besieged to fight alone the war of dreamers.

But sometimes late at night men dance undaunted towards hope
Beholden to a task that feeds the soul with fertile whispers
And amidst that motley crew I measured words like precious diamonds
Brazen gems I hoped would prove immortal prose.

I chose the writer's path of fearless letters charged with love
Believing they could etch their truth in a heart more steadfast than stone
Another arrogant wordsmith determined to freeze fresh petals on the stem
If not forever, then at least for you, as a perfect rose today.

Apex

the light of a legend
is there in your eyes
the fragrance of moonlight
enhances your sighs

while laurels of glory
compete for the rest
the challenge you promise
is my sacred test

a reason perfected
to fight against Death
determined beside you
to savor each breath

as Time taps undaunted
each ominous tick
my heartbeat is humbled
by moments too quick

and I would choose nothing
if I could not find
your love at the summit
for you I must climb.

Hallow Hopes

If the meeting of our eyes
could burn the magic of your memory
into the creases of my mind
forever more,
exact and complete,
a perfect facsimile,
believe me when I say
I would not hesitate
to embrace that searing brand;
for such is the desperate strength of my desire
to capture this fleeting moment,
and preserve it complete,
till death calls me home.

Through

When our heart's finest words have been spoken
In loving whispers & frightened tongues
I will gather the fragments of our favorite conversations together
Blending piles of tender memories
With shards of the precious times we shared
Beholden forever to the echoes of you that keep me awake.

When sorrow seems infinite as if there is no more than this
A jagged hollow within & a perfect circle without
Both spaces empty yet complete
I will remember your face & my eyes will melt
I will say your name & my breath will be spent
I will savor your touch like a warm prairie sunset.

When I stagger under the weight of mortal delusions
Asking "why" although the nature of things is clear
I will find less blame than unwanted answers
Behind the pillars of my pain
And some relief in the knowledge
That you no longer suffer such common angst.

When my arms are empty I will still hold onto you
Though not for want of comfort or protection
At last there is nothing left to fear
The body expires but our love is immortal
So I will dance naked in the forest for both of us
Gather eagle feathers to restore my wings
And surrender to the promise of everyone's tomorrow
Knowing that here or there, we will be together forever

Seedlings of Grace
&
In-sight

All Strung Out

These moments together, a necklace of snowflakes
Pure crystalline magic, all perfect and new

So laugh love and savor, the memories unfolding

For blessings like these, are remarkably few.

The first rays of morning, the moon's gentle kiss

The sweet taste of passion, all virtuous bliss

A dream born in heaven, a smile without shame

Past glories remembered, the sound of Love's name.

Thus mentioned a handful, of life's greatest rhythms

Immaculate chapters, with pages of sand

For one fragile instant, perfection is written

By we who are cradled, in Destiny's hand.

Capture & Rapture

From wind-tickled meadows & fantasy fare

To dreams out of reach you are hungry to share

Laughing angels are dancing beyond space and time

On the shimmering pinnacles U wish U would climb

To conquer the moment your heartbeat explains

That all glory transcendent is mirrored with pain

From the grace of a miracle wrapped in a star

To the promise fulfilled by a fertile bazaar

There is ever a price for the freedom we seek

Like the challenges faced by both strong & the weak

And if web is the word for the love of a deed

Then ensnared U shall be when U answer your need.

It is one's purpose,
not power,
that makes a man
great.

GarthSam(c) 2019

uno

you know,

for the beacon that guides your soul shines a way through
the darkness;

and yet you would suffer blindness rather than face the
light;

stumble uncertainly rather than dance unencumbered;

lose your way in the maze, although gracefully guided;

for with in-sight comes Understanding,

and none borne to see clearly can escape her peerless
caress.

you know,

so why do you run to find places where you cannot hide?

instead, seek your peace in faith knowing:

like the love of the earth for the fruit that it bears

all roads,

shall in time,

lead you back,

to just One.

c/me

I am flushed with a unified purpose
Fully bound to the calling of Light
Though I sway I return to the center
Where my fate is to challenge the night.

Equidistant the space all around me
thus I inhale my breath from the whole
As I stretch up to siphon the darkness
time consumes me yet flatters my goal.

Liquid flavors that tease me are fragile
complementing the rhymes that I sing
For we both know the secret of passion
is surrender to change that it brings.

I would dance for a time without knowing,
when my promise would have me released
For the flame that I am was born knowing
only grace lights the candle of peace.

Mind no Matter

The time has come to realize, the dream you seek to be:
To activate the latent force, & set your power free.

No more the speaker of a wish, upon a distant star
For now you choose to redefine, the way in which you are.

To wrest from apathetic grip, control of thought and form
Transcending disempowered states, so easily the norm.

Inhale each morning's fire-light, inspired to be alive
your greatness craves expression & it shall not be denied.

*

Undeniable the offer, irrefutable the claim
As momentum speaks to motion, so beginnings herald change

Let your will be sharply focused, let no evil make you doubt
That the goal you are pursuing, you were meant to do without

Face your fears & be reminded, of the greatest deeds you've done
Stretch towards your finest moments, bravely claim a higher rung.

Thus take notice of this summons & put talent to the test
Have no doubt when mind meets matter you are called
to be your best.

Until when

To live the unbreakable moment.
To climb the unscalable wall.
To reach for the top of the mountain.
To heed the unlimited call.

To master the rhyme & the reason.
To treasure the gift that is yours.
To stand up for what you believe in.
To savor the sand as it pours.

To gratefully go where you're needed.
To marry forgiveness with faith.
To never take beauty for granted.
To search for the meaning of grace.

To know that the music of laughter
Is the best song to sing with your friends.
And Time offers all the same counsel:
To be present from now until when.

Fear Less

I would carve marble by sheer force of will
Move a mountain rather than stumble over it
Never fall though I leap from solid ground into the void
And draw breath underwater by pure intent to do so

These are the forces I wield and rely on
Sewn together with both sinew and soul-matter
Thus empowered I call myself master of Time
Though seconds laugh so indifferent to my grasp.

Still deny any limits if it is possible to do so
See no obstacle as greater than you can pass
When we believe in our presence and purpose
Naught will stop us from a life without fear.

just so.

The dreams that you seek
are there warmly before you
true allies indeed
of the great cosmic game

The sound that your ears
have been straining to capture
is simply the wind as it
echoes your name

The sights you would treasure
as visions of glory
are sprinkled in mirrors
for all eyes to see

The taste so delicious
your appetite chases
is only the flavor
of who you could be

*

Ask where does it come from?
this bountiful harvest
and gather your thoughts
as the sun gathers rain

For within the question
so richly examined
your faith shares the answer
again and again.

A Stitch in Rhyme

In a field of bright flowers I savor the feeling

of being embraced by the power of light

A solar son planted here, gathering wisdom

From all seven senses that conquer the night.

With golden discoveries & sweet understanding

The knowledge of contact between one & all

I watch as a blossom floats gently towards me

And smile as I share in the grace of its fall.

Re-View

Consider here a different view of how your life could be
Unfettered by the silly things that make you less than free
A novel way to greet the dawn, a fresh approach at night
Perspective shifted so you see the warmest rays of light.

It may seem both mysterious & fickle at the start
Because alas we're often told to play a minor part
But if you care to take a dare & step outside the box
You'll find the sand on which U stand is sown with sacred rocks.

A gift of steps to guide the few who seek less traveled paths
Wise ways & means to savor grace & bypass Karma's wrath
Within the hearts of those who choose to dance instead of crawl
Reside the tools for kings & fools to share the best of all.

For once our basic needs are met, the rest need not be hard
If work & play reflect each day the wisdom of the bard
When gratitude pays homage to humility not shame
You too can skew the odds of life towards a winning game.

And for the odd who must refuse to settle like the rest
The brave & the uncommon men who pass Life's fickle test
A destiny awaits that guarantees a job well-done
For s/he who has the least regrets is ever s/he who won.

T. for 2

Some men will sell you loyalty
But all must give their trust
That perfect gift without a price
Though offer if you must
Your dollars & your diamonds both
What riches you would spend
You cannot buy your way within
The fortress of a friend
Those golden walls impregnable
A haven pure & true
So safe within the heart of trust
The unprotected You
Unburdened by suspicious thoughts
Released from fear & shame
In comfort & security
No need to levy blame
For poor indeed are those who live
Eternally in doubt
And never know the honest grace
Of company without,
Grey motives, false sincerity
Self-interest at the core
Instead of just the wind beneath
Your wings to make you soar
Rethink then as you gauge your wealth
If trust you do not "own"
For riches cannot slake the thirst
Of s/he who drinks alone.

Search & Rescue

Fate, time, and rainbows are much like the concepts
Your heart would embrace if your soul knew the way
In honor of instinct you wisely are seeking
A guide who will help you unravel the maze.

Someone with knowledge of more than a taste or two
Rich with the flavor of life's heady draught
She who inspires you to scale your Everest
He who is dancing on Joy's sacred path.

Light is no burden to those who shun darkness
As Time yields politely to dreams born of love
Peace finds expression through silence and kindness
While glory sings softly of gifts from above.

You who are eager to shape-shift your energy
You who require more meaning than proof
Walk to the rhythm of purpose in purity
Satisfy hunger with banquets of truth.

Ode to the SHERO

YOU ARE a SHERO!
Bent often but never broken.
You have fallen many times, but you are still standing.
A goddess remembering the power within
not the problems without.
Fierce with the faith of a mother's love
and blessed with the strength of a sister.
You are forever inspired to be more tomorrow
Than you could be yesterday.

YOU ARE a SHERO!
Undeniably worthy of expressing your very best
despite any cruel or insecure efforts by those
who might dare to deny, deprive
diminish or discredit you.
No.
You will permit NO ONE to limit your light
With either deeds of darkness
Or words of dishonesty.

YOU ARE a SHERO!
Your destiny is to align with only the greatest good.
Unfettered & undaunted
inspired by the beauty of every sacred sunrise
and humbled by the timeless guidance of the moon
you too are an indomitable force of nature
and your heart wields the power of love.

YOU ARE a SHERO
Above the din,
despite the distractions
more courageous than your challenges
you command respect:
for you are a Wonder-full Woman who was born to shine
and your life will be no less than PHENOMENAL!

161

Supra-Nova

Seek ye the grace of still waters
Let peace rule the heights that you reach
Speak of the truth as you know it
And strive to be more than you teach.

Rise to the challenge of sharing
The light of your soulfire best
And shine with the love you embody
A starchild & more but not less.

Onward & Upward

Look up...
When you carry a hard day to bed.
Look up...
When kinder words *should* have been said.
Look up...
When your dreams are caught in the rain.
Look up...
When Life writes you a diary of pain.
Look up...
When you start to believe wrong is right.
Look up...
When you question the power of Light.
Look up...
When you suffer the sadness of death.
Look up...
When you struggle for one more breath.
Look up...
To remember how far you have grown
Look up...
To be proud of the seeds you have sown.
Look up...
To remember the best deeds you've done
Look up...
And find faith in a kiss from the sun.

Sometimes our lives are reframed
by our experiences.
Sometimes our options are obscured.
Sometimes we are overwhelmed
by the waves...
And sometimes we are lifted
higher by them.

GarthSam(c)2015

Makedancing 101

Could it be that what you're missing?
Is just waiting to be found

In the wake of meditations
On the sublime and profound?

When the mind is unencumbered
There is never any doubt

That a state of dark confusion
We may choose to live without.

Like a cloudless sky breathes sunshine,
Understanding offers light

As the pulse of morning quickens
At the passing of the night.

There's a freedom born of knowing
Brighter days are yet to come

Once the door is jimmied open
Logarithmic is the sum

Of both clarity and greatness
No more need for hidden games:

Vision graduates through blindness
At the sound of Wisdom's name.

Thus the circle is expanded
From the edges to the core

And believers feel the music
As they dance from less to more.

Momentous Occasions

I choose now to savor

A taste of those flavors

That make life not bitter but sweet:

And dance for a time

To the joy of a rhyme

And the happiness born of a beat.

A Call to the Conscious

No wicked are chosen, to shine as if golden
For they lack the light, that makes heroes of men
Still others possess, talent more than the rest
But let fear steal their power, again & again.

Then too there are those, born to preen and to pose
Who believe that perception, is equal the part
As if surface traits, stand as proof of true grace
When their soul is a window, exposing the dark.

Thus written the adage, withstanding Time's passage
That while some are called, very few make the grade
But those who stand worthy, of more than vain glory
Share blood, sweat & time, as the price they have paid.

So what of your quest, to be one of the best
Who enjoy more than most & come ready to dance
Prepare for each task, leave the past in the past
And place more faith in choice, than the whimsy of chance.

Blindsighted

It is only our perspective
that separates us from one another's dreams

Those gauzy filters through which we see
ALL the world go by

No exceptions or delays regardless
whether diamond, mud or vapor

Time is a glutton
for the taste of every single second.

No doubt it would be best then
to see it simply like smoke in the wind

For as fast as we draw first breath
so too do we exhale for the very last time

And with so many ways to meet the dark night
This freefall is far more fragile than most can imagine

Still we have only these precious moments to entertain us
In the space between shadows and doubts.

So for better than worse our Fate is to cling and to chase
To celebrate and to mourn

As happy hopes help us believe it will all be ok
When in fact it could not be any other way.

no competition

YOU control the passion – YOU control the heat
YOU control the rhythm – YOU control the beat
YOU control the sunshine – YOU control the rain
YOU control the losses – YOU control the gain
YOU control the envy – YOU control the greed
YOU control the hunger – YOU control the need
YOU control the purpose – YOU control the flame
YOU control the sweepstakes – YOU control the game
YOU control the volume – YOU control the noise
YOU control the fashion – YOU control the poise
YOU control the tempo – YOU control the pace
YOU control the setting – YOU control the space.

YOU can reap the magic – born with every dawn
YOU can climb the mountain – once your fear is gone
Search for sage solutions – live a noble creed
Dance away from darkness – plant a loving seed
This is just a channel – this is not the song
YOU must write the title – whether short or long
From a fertile vessel – comes an ageless voice
YOU remain the master - yours is still the choice
Live a new direction – take a different course
Best is freely chosen – all words flow from source
Shape a greater vision – see with clearer eyes
Yearn to marry freedom – live to win the prize.

Well-sprung

How deep would you drink from a well-full of wisdom?
How much would you eat from a table of truth?
How long would you listen to songs of sincerity
Those plaintive & candid expressions of youth?

Look not just to one side nor only the middle
Your center is neither the spot nor the state
But rather the answer to this daunting riddle
What mettle or manner enhances one's fate?

Adamantium will bound to resolute footsteps?
A diamond-hard nature that won't accept "no"?
A blast-furnace character blazing with passion?
A heart bound to purpose & eager to grow?

Or could it be simply as meek are made heroes
That there is no option for any to choose
Apart from the role we are cast in from zero
All men play a game that no man wants to lose.

So bend back for buckets & draw up the ocean
Gorge like a man starving & savor the feast
Choose music or silence to help you discover
The way or the well-spring that best offers peace.

Primary Colors

The colors we blend for our palette
Are the colors that govern our lives
The paint we apply through our effort
Creates art as each moment arrives.

The master is s/he who is willing
Using brushstrokes both bold and refined
To explore the ripe depths of the rainbow
For the treasures therein s/he will find.

So inquire of yourself are you ready
To unveil that which lies in your heart
To believe in the masterpiece waiting
For all those who pursue life as art.

Reasons to Believe

In times like these that beg for humble heroes
To stanch wounds & mend broken fences
Are you not also a warrior-in-waiting
Queued to join the fray & battle the madness?

We share more sights of sadness than ever before
This digital season is ripe with inspiring images
Without eyes closed & ears stopped
It is impossible to pretend that all is well for many.

But hiding from the truth is not what truly moves you
You know that it is always better to do more than nothing
And while no one can give what they do not have
The spirit thrives best when we practice compassion.

Between moments of doubt & despair that test your faith
Do not be discouraged by the wickedness of shallow men
Their legacy is the dirt no one wants to remember
And humanity never mourns the death of a shadow.

You were not taught to be callous or indifferent
You were born to make the world a better place
The only reason not to help those who are suffering
Is the cold decision not to care enough.

There has never been a better time than now to lean in
For every great shift only happens when we do
And as you shine brightly to beat back the darkness
You become another brave reason for us all to believe.

Tao

It does exist, that core defining center
A pure reward for those who match the scales
And realize, with pride but without balance
A "master's" expert wisdom also fails.

For Harmony knows only that which tends it
Shall earn the gentle harvest she bestows
While all else blindly planted in her garden
Yields conflict and confusion as it grows.

So why endure the bristles of discomfort
When peace is there for seekers to embrace?
Abandon patterns shown to be lopsided
In favor of a balanced state of grace.

Clear & Present

I shall not try to force these days

Nor charge them with a mission out of context

Their will shall be their own

To dance in defiance of the moving Truth

That here today will always be gone tomorrow

Evaporatus maximus, the Grand Eternal

For Time alone lasts

while we who see will not for long

So eyes wide hearts open souls ready

Today this dreamscape is as defiant as diamond

And far more precious indeed as naught but ALL:

The shining Present.

TARGET PRACTICE

Harness your unbridled passion.

Conquer your limiting fears.

Search for a consummate purpose.

Grow beyond cloudy to clear.

There is a season for solitude.

There is a reason for faith.

Now is the moment you've waited for.

Here is the time and the place.

See Do Be

For us all the journey begins with insight
A glimpse at first through a pore of possibility
That widens sooner or later into a vista of fate
We carve as fast as we crave to see our selves
Unfettered by doubts or distractions
The limitations of ambivalence are as thick as blue shadows
And we are wont to will what we witness
On the other side of the mirror
That is where the truth is waiting
For that is where the heart is beating
Not the shell or the polish
Just the raw essence of an original adventure
Ready and willing to be written
When the seer knows what s/he seeks
Then the door flies open on seamless hinges
And mountains become meadows
Thoughts that once teased no longer tickle
Instead they seize the day
As inner forces align with outer choices
To boldly claim the ultimate gift
Beyond rewards and accolades only one thing truly matters:
Knowing who you are and what you were born to do.

The Inspiration of Prophets

I see between the lines of your affliction
and recognize the limits of your goal
I trace the changing contours of your passion
to gently soothe the aching of your soul.

Do you possess the strength to stand beside me
unwrapped as if I knew you like a son?
And are you brave enough to seek truth only
If so, there is no other race to run.

All naked are we born to spin through moments
with reins of hope we try to tame the ride
So tell me if you wish to know the answer
why is it you so often choose to hide?

A dignity of spirit is enlightened
the blessed hear the rhythm of a dream
All those with whom the word becomes united
shall realize the visions they have seen.

Walking Words

You are not here simply
to retrace the dusty footprints of another

Nor have you come solely
to sing the high praises of your brother.

Although each loss provides guidance
from consequences too bold to deny

Only a fool would trade success for failure
When winds of fate would see them fly.

Extract instead the knowledge gained
at your considerable expense

Then march towards the finish line,
inspired from that time hence.

Though the wealth of kings & moguls
may elude your efforts still

If virtue guides your steps have faith;
in time your heart will earn its fill.

ICARUS RISING

Are you prepared to abandon your broken ways,

open your heart to the dream meant for you?

Is there a place in your soul for a remedy,

borne on the wings of the deeds you could do?

Bask in the promise of change & new symmetry.

Laugh at the sight of the shadows you wore.

Share in the sound of a genuine symphony.

Simply decide to believe & to soar.

Those who can see...
may know.
Those who cannot...
may be shown.

Those who will not...
must suffer their karma.

GarthSam(c)2015

Perfect Prose

Everyone is called to bear the weight of their destiny

But it is not simply a matter of discharging daily tasks & deeds.

The mantle of divine duty is both a yoke of great responsibility

And a grace-full opportunity for self-realization.

Yin always balances yang to express the whole truth

As even the loftiest flight ultimately succumbs to gravity.

For though we wish to only soar untroubled

Soap-bubble moments remain the cousins of cannonballs

Falling with as little apology as those diaphanous spheres
pop in the sunlight.

Thus passion is tempered by Fate and all dreams defer to karma

While we shoulder our burdens and savor our blessings

Comic or tragic, the stories we live are always soul-perfect.

Will to Shine

Shake off the layers of your homely confusion
The dirt on a diamond does not help it shine:
You must believe that your will & your talents
Are all that you need for the stars to align.

Doubtful you wonder if effort means anything
Or whether karma is written in time.
One truth stands out in your search for an answer:
Only with step after step do we climb.

Into the darkness where pride becomes folly
Character grows when the soul meets the night:
Those who press on through the pain & the shadows
Earn the rewards for their valiant fight.

Be not like fools who rush straight into battle
Wise Men take time choosing how-to & when:
With patience & prudence the sage is undaunted
The brave & determined find their means to an end.

So hone your instincts & deepen your discipline
We all start with talent but few possess skill:
Do not live weakly to die soon forgotten
Instead shape your fate with your grit & your will.

onE daY magneT

recumbent beneath the heavens

i feast on azure manna

rich soul food for a dreamer

who plays games with the stars.

each perfect micro-moment

dazzling & indifferent

is an opus to the eternal continuum

and my gratitude is boundless.

what then is more wholesome

than to match beauty with mysterious hope

and savor love from the source

of all things truly sublime.

Weighs and Means

The true measure of a man lies not in the cut of his clothes,
the style of his fashion, or the cost of his accessories,
but rather in the dignity with which he dresses himself,
and the honor that he wears daily.

The true measure of a man has far less to do
with the title that he holds professionally
than the respect that he inspires personally,
from those who seek both his company and his counsel.

The true measure of a man is not his net worth
counted in dollars and cents,
but his net wisdom made manifest by the grace of his conduct,
the harmony of his relations, and the integrity of his words.

The true measure of a man is not to be found simply
in a survey of who he knows,
but instead in the sublime expression of how well
he knows himself as a child of the Universe,
and the depth of his surrender to the infinite Divine.

The true measure of a man is gracefully revealed
in the purity of his love,
the nobility of his actions,
the generosity of his nature,
and the tranquility of his spirit.